Toddler Potty Training:

Incredibly Simple 2-Day Potty Training that Works

Marie C. Foster

Table of Contents

Introduction:

The first year of your baby's life is incredible, as you marvel in all the developmental milestones that they achieve. It is beautiful watching your little one as they learn to pick up their head, then crawl, and start to explore the world around them. Something you must consider as they age, however, is the right time to start potty training.

Toilet training can be separated into two separate approaches. The first is the 'wait-for-your-toddler-to-be-ready' approach, which is generally a lot longer than early potty training. The second is teaching your kid when you believe they are developmentally ready. There are numerous advantages to this, including an easier and quicker training process (because your child has not yet developed bad habits like stubbornness or getting used to the feeling of pee or poop in their diaper), a higher level of self-esteem and independence for your child, and less money spent on diapers over your child's lifetime.

Once you realize that the best method is to get your child ready for potty training, instead of waiting for them to be ready, the next step is to read through the pages of this book. If you are a busy parent, this 2-day method is ideal. You can choose to potty train your toddler in a single weekend, rather than needing to find the time to stretch it over three days, as is common with the 3-day method.

In this book, you are going to learn how to prepare yourself (and your little one) for toddler potty training. You will learn what to buy beforehand, the best methods of convincing your son or daughter to climb onto the potty, and how to reward them, to make sure that using the toilet becomes a habit.

For parents who have spoken to others about potty training, heard horror stories or developed struggles of their own, skepticism might be at the front of their minds when they hear that the toddler potty training method only takes two days. However, as a parent who has tried this method out personally, I can say that it really does work. The two-day method was effective and while it did require a great deal of commitment the weekend that I put it into practice, it was well worth it. By the end of the weekend, my toddler was a potty trained champ!

Truthfully, even if you are skeptical, there is almost nothing to lose from trying this method. You will purchase the things that you would have to purchase when your child was ready anyway, like underwear and a potty chair. Aside from these costs, the only thing that you must commit to the process is your time. Since it is designed to fit into a single weekend, this is hardly a sacrifice.

So, what do you have to lose? Prepare yourselves and gear up for the next weekend you have free and make it all about getting your little one to put their pee and poop where it belongs. It is a small time commitment that is well worth it.

Best of luck on your potty training journey!

Chapter 1: Getting Started with Toddler Potty Training

Chapter 1: Getting Started with Toddler Potty Training

Children become toddlers when they reach certain developmental milestones between 1 and 2 years of age. It is during this time when they may start moving around more, try (and eventually succeed) at walking, and start expanding their vocabulary. The toddler stage is also characterized by an increased awareness of the child's surroundings, a desire for great independence, recognition of the toddler's own person and that of others, imitation of behavior and even defiant behavior. While this milestone means many things, it can also indicate that your child is ready to start toddler potty training.

What is Toddler Potty Training?

Toddler potty training does not really relate to a specific age of potty training. Typically, it takes place before the child indicates being ready, which is common when parents take the more relaxed approach to toilet training. Toddler potty training describes any toilet training that is initiated by the parent, though it usually takes place between 1 and 2 years of age.

When Should I Start Toddler Potty Training?

It is entirely up to you when you start potty training. You should note, however, that your child should be able to do several things before you start the process. Before starting, make sure that your toddler can:

- Walk to the toilet or potty training chair
- Say at least a few words, indicating that they can communicate with you when they have to go to the toilet
- Show that he/she wants to please you, or at least has a potty-training receptive attitude

If your child has reached these developmental milestones, then your little one may be ready for potty training.

The 3-Day Method of Toilet Training vs. the 2-Day Methods

One of the most popular methods of potty training is the 3-day method, which gives your toddler an extra day to work on getting the potty technique down to a fine art. Unfortunately, not all parents can work with the 3-day method, especially those who work during the week or who have busy lifestyles. While many of the techniques used are similar, doing the work in 2 days lets you schedule it in for the weekend.

Why Toilet Training Your Toddler is Important

Some parents and experts recommend that you allow your child to start potty training when ready. You should familiarize them with the toilet and praise them if they want to use it, but generally, allow the toddler to decide when they are ready themselves.

The problem with the 'wait-until-your-child-is-ready' method of potty training is that it can take significantly longer to convince your child to start using the toilet.

This is okay for some families, but it does restrict what your child can do. For example, most preschools and some daycares require that a child is potty trained before attending. This lets the teachers and caregivers give all the children the attention and time that is needed for learning, rather than spending their time worrying about which child needs to use the bathroom.

Benefits of Early Toilet Training

In some cultures and the western world specifically, it has become a popular trend to let children decide when they are ready to potty train, rather than encouraging them early on. Early toilet training does not include training as an infant, but takes place between the ages of 1 and 2, once the child meets the right developmental milestones. This is considered early because the waiting method usually takes place after 2 ½ years of age. Some of the benefits of encouraging your child to potty train sooner include:

- Less Time to Form Bad Habits- As your toddler becomes more self-aware, the child will start to recognize the sensations of peeing and pooping inside their diaper. This familiarity becomes detrimental the longer that you wait to potty train them because they will become comfortable having the waste inside their pants. This habit can be hard to break, especially when they are more interested in things like eating, watching television or playing rather than taking the few minutes break needed to use the restroom.

- Less Defiance- The younger a child is, the more likely it is that they will respond well to their parents' encouragement during toilet training. After two, toddlers tend to become more defiant and less likely to care about pleasing, as they start to challenge their parents' authority and push boundaries. This newfound defiance does not stop as they age, so teaching your toddler before he or she enters this stage can greatly increase the likelihood of success.

- Better Awareness of Bowel Signals- Not only does peeing and pooping in a diaper become a habit as your toddler ages, so does ignoring the signals that the body sends when it needs to eliminate waste. This makes it less likely that your child will pay attention enough to the signals to stop what they are doing at the time and use the toilet.

In addition to avoiding some of the unpleasant effects of waiting too long to potty train your toddler, here are some advantages:

- Lowers the Cost of Parenting- When you train your child to use the bathroom earlier, you ultimately spend less money on diapers and pull-ups. The method described in this book does not recommend the use of pull-ups at all, so it will drastically reduce the amount you spend on diapers throughout your child's life.

- Lowers Impact on the Environment- Did you know that the average disposable diaper can lie around for 500 years before decomposing? Not only are you saving money by purchasing fewer diapers, you are contributing to the environment in a positive way.

- Improves Self-Esteem and Independence- As your child matures, they will take pleasure in their milestones and development. This is especially true as you praise them. By teaching your child to potty train earlier, you can increase their sense of capability and independence. This, in turn, increases their self-esteem and confidence.

- Benefits Your Child's Health and Hygiene- With potty training should come positive hygiene habits like hand washing. This encourages good health. Additionally, you have to worry less about irritation and diaper rash once your child is no longer sitting in wet diapers for a long period of time.

- More Flexibility for Daycare and School- If your child is not toilet trained, you may find that certain daycares and schools will not accept them as a student. If your child already has good bathroom habits, you will not have to stress about how long they are sitting in their diaper at the daycare or if they will be accepted to preschool.

Overview of the 2-Day Potty Training Method

As you read this book, we will go over how to train your 2-year old in detail. Before we get started, here are the basic steps you can expect.

1. Preparing Your Child for Potty Training- Before you get started, you will need a specific strategy to teach your child to use the toilet.

2. Teaching Toilet Communication- If your child cannot tell you that they need to pee or poop, it will be very hard for them to start potty training.

3. Introducing Your Child to the Toilet- Before your child will willingly sit on the potty, you must teach them about the toilet and what it is for.

4. Applying the 2-Day Method of Potty Training- This will go over

potty training boot camp, where your child will learn all the skills they need to stay dry during the day.

In addition to details about the 2-day potty training process above, you will learn the best way to get your child to stay diaper free, common mistakes that you should avoid for toilet training success and bonus tips for girls, boys and dads.

CHAPTER SUMMARY:

1. Toddler potty training describes any early training initiated by the parent, rather than waiting for cues from the child that he or she is ready.

Usually, this occurs between the first and second years of a child's life, when the toddler can communicate, is able to walk to the toilet, and has a willing attitude toward doing what their caregiver requests. That is when the 2-day method will be most effective.

2. There are many benefits for the 2-day method when compared against the wait-for-the-toddler method. Toddlers are often more eager to please during this time and have not yet developed 'bad' potty habits, like ignoring their bodily signals that they have to pee or poop or sitting in a dirty diaper. Additionally, you save

money on diapers and lessen your impact on the environment.

3. The 2-day potty training technique is ideal for parents who have a busy schedule and need to fit the training into a 2-day weekend. By committing your time, you will easily be able to use the procedure described in this book to convince your toddler to use the toilet.

YOUR QUICK START ACTION STEP: FIND MORE INFORMATION

If you do not want to skim the pages of this book, or you have a question that has not been answered yet, find out a little more about the 2-day method of potty training by reading at least one website. You can also compare methods if you would like to, to see which technique is best for you and your child.

Chapter 2:
Potty Training
Preparation

Chapter 2: Potty Training Preparation

Potty training is not something that will happen without work. You cannot 'wing it' or just do it. Rather, toilet training is something that you must plan for. You will need to buy a few things to set your child up for success and have a well-thought-out, strategic plan of action to get potty training done over the weekend.

Why You Need a Strategic Plan for Potty Training

Let me tell you why 'just doing it' is a mistake. My son was around

15 months old when he showed an interest in the potty for the first time. As a new parent, I was excited. I could hardly believe that it would be that simple. I jumped into it with both feet, giving him plenty of praise each time that he went on the potty and asking him several times a day if he needed to go.

While I thought this would be enough, we lacked a lot of consistency. The times that I did catch him were flukes and, months later, he was still not fully trained. Some days, he would not go on the toilet at all because we were busy and he still did not understand how to ask to use the potty.

Had I taken the time to do a little more research, I probably would have had a much easier time potty training. I was fortunate enough with my daughter that I had already done the research for her brother. When she showed interest around 17 months, we tried the 2-day method and it went off without a hitch. In a single weekend, she had learned what it took almost a year for our son to learn.

Benefits of Developing a Strategic Potty Training Plan

Strategic planning comes with many benefits that make it ideal in any situation, not just while toilet training. Even so, here are some ways that coming up with a clear potty training plan can help get your child on track:

- Clear End Goal- When you plan, you can see the end goal very clearly. Following this 2-day crash course, the ideal situation is that your child becomes familiar enough with the toilet that they choose not to go to the bathroom in their underpants. Ideally, you should be able to leave them in underwear and not worry too much about accidents. They may happen from time to time, but the goal of potty training is to minimize them.

- Establishing Direction- Once you know where the end goal is, you can establish the direction that you want potty training to take. This includes the way that you introduce and describe the toilet to your toddler. Make sure as you do this that you are clear about your expectations that you expect them to go pee and poop in the toilet from now on.

- Offering Consistent Rewards- One of the biggest problems I had when training my first son was inconsistency, both with rewards and going to the bathroom. When you develop a strategic plan and put it into action, the rewards (and the message you are trying to send your toddler) is consistent.

- Clearing the Weekend- Once you have a plan, you can choose a timeframe to do it in. Stock up on snacks, juice and anything else you need to get through the weekend and keep your toddler at home. You can have visitors over, but be sure to stick to the potty training schedule regardless of who is around. Consistently paying attention to your little one's 'potty' signals and regularly getting them on the toilet is critical if you want to have success with the 2-day method.

- Giving Your Toddler Goals- One of the great things that comes along with potty training is boosted self-esteem and independence. If you come up with a goal and share it with your toddler, they are going to revel in their accomplishments, too. They are going to know exactly what you expect them to do and when they find themselves capable of it, they will have a newfound confidence and gratification in potty training.

How to Develop a Toddler Potty Training Strategy

Now, you know that planning is critical to toilet training success, it's time to go over the steps that will get you there. Coming up with a strategy is not just jotting down a few ideas on a piece of paper and calling it done. Follow this process for success with your strategic planning.

1. Do Your Research- If you followed the quick-action plan suggested at the end of the first chapter, you might have already had a jumpstart on this. The first thing that you should do is check

out a few different potty training strategies. For parents who are worried about their child going potty on the carpet, consider choosing a warm day and letting your little one run around naked in the backyard. As you choose the methods that you implement, however, keep in mind your toddler's personality and what will be most effective for him or her and least stressful for you. Doing this gives you the greatest chance of toilet training success.

2. Decide What Plan to Implement- After plenty of research, you will have a clear picture of the many techniques that can be used for potty training. Once you have decided,

move onto the next steps of planning.

3. The Great Underwear Debate- One of the biggest horrors of toilet training is the realization that your little one's pee and poop is not going to be contained by a diaper. Pull-ups can work for some children, but they are less likely to work because they are so close to being a diaper. Even the ones with the cool-touch that happens when your child pees or poops may not cause them to understand the relations between the bladder and bowel movement and understand how it feels when they have to go. For this reason, many people recommend moving straight to underwear with potty

training. If you do choose this, make sure to stack up on plenty of undies before the big weekend.

4. Stock Up on Rewards- Before you get started, you will have to decide how you want to reward your little one for their efforts. Choose a small candy (like chocolate chips), stickers, or something else your toddler is interested in. You should also prepare yourself to be available for plenty of praise to go with whatever treat that you choose as a reward. It can also be helpful to differentiate between pees and poops by offering a second small candy or a large sticker rather than a small one for when your toddler does number two. Put off

visits to the park and grandma's house and go shopping before you start the potty training journey. This way, there will be no distractions from toilet training.

6. Communicate with Your Toddler- It is best to potty train after you have had at least a few days to get your child excited about the weekend to come. Always explain the upcoming toilet training crash course as something exciting that you are going to do together. You could also take him/her to the bathroom with you, their other parent, or an older sibling, so they can see how their role models use their toilet.

7. Get it done- Once you have considered all these areas, its time to write out the plan. Decide what you need to buy and prepare your toddler for the upcoming weekend, by showing plenty of excitement.

CHAPTER SUMMARY:

1. Developing a strategic plan for potty training is critical to toilet training success. If you try to implement toilet training without a plan, you may lack the consistency that is necessary to make your little one start using the toilet. Having a plan lets you prepare better, develop consistency and focus on the end

goal, all of which are going to improve your efforts.

2. When you fail to plan, you plan to fail. By coming up with a strategy that will work for you and your toddler, you ultimately set yourselves up for potty training success. Additionally, you gain the benefits of knowing exactly what to do over the upcoming weekend and are able to prepare, so you do not have to leave the house during boot camp.

3. You can come up with a descriptive toilet training strategy in 7 simple steps. Remember to consider your child's personality as you develop the strategy for optimal success. Then, decide on

factors like whether you will use underwear or pull-ups (or let them wear nothing at all), when the potty training will take place, and how your child will communicate and be rewarded each time that they need to go.

YOUR QUICK START ACTION STEP: KEEP LEARNING

Spend several minutes checking out different potty training techniques as was suggested in Step 1. This will prepare you to come up with a strategic plan that works, rather than choosing one and hoping for the best. Once you have done this and decided what method to use, turn the page to the next chapter and start the next step of the 2-day potty training journey.

Chapter 3:

Proper Communication Tips

Chapter 3: Proper Communication Tips

Picture this. It is 1950s America and disposable diapers have yet to hit the shelves. Each time that your little one decides to soil his or her cloth diaper, you must rinse or scrub the diaper, as well as your toddler's bottom. This is a tiring and tedious process, one that you would like to do as little as possible.

The only logical solution during these earlier days was to potty train—early. Each time that the baby went in the toilet represented another cloth diaper that didn't need to be rinsed and washed. These small victories would lead to potty training much earlier than is the standard now— by the age of 2.

One of the reasons credited by doctors is because children are not emotionally ready for toilet training until they are between 2 and 3. The fast-paced lifestyle that many parents lead may also be to blame, as time being a parent, working, and attending to the many commitments that come along with having children take up time. Even so, it is not uncommon for younger children to be toilet trained—it is common practice for children in Eastern Europe, Asia, Latin America and Africa to have their children toilet trained by 2 years of age.

This proves that it is possible to communicate with your child, even when they are in the earlier years of their life. This chapter will teach you about why this communication is important and how you can develop potty training communication between yourself and your toddler. This will lead to toilet training success.

What is Successful Toilet Training Communication?

Successful potty training communication describes a communication relationship that goes both ways. You must communicate what you want your toddler to do in a way that they understand and are willing.

However, you must also be receptive to the communication signals that your toddler is sending out to you.

When I was potty training my youngest, we spent plenty of time on doing research before the big weekend. We wanted to take the proper steps, so we didn't develop the same problems with her that we had with our son. One thing that we paid close attention to leading up to the big day was her pottying habits. Even though she didn't know the words yet, our daughter was letting us know with her body movements when she needed to go. It almost seemed like she was embarrassed about pooping because she would go into a corner or hide under a table before doing her business. She also still got the 'shivers' that babies sometimes get following a pee. Once we recognized the signals that she was sending us, we could teach her the words for pee and poop.

I think the communication between myself and our daughter was a big help in the process. She learned to identify them as 'ee' and 'oo' (she couldn't pronounce a 'P' sound yet) and we responded by getting her to the potty as quickly as possible. After a few rounds of this, she started to head toward the toilet herself, shrieking 'ee' or 'oo' on her way.

We were fortunate enough to recognize our daughter's signals early on, which gave us a jumpstart on communication. Even if you aren't sure where to start, this chapter is going to teach you what you need to know. By the end, you will have the steps necessary to create a positive result connecting and communicating with your toddler as you potty train.

Why Communication is Important

Have you ever heard a word you were unfamiliar with? You probably never came across it before, nor have you heard it said by someone else. In this situation, you either asked what the other person meant or used context clues to figure out what was going on.

Your child's brain is much less-developed than that of an adult. As your toddler learns and grows, they form connections in the brain that relate certain sensations and feelings to the words that you give them. When you begin potty training, it is unlikely that your child associates the feeling of peeing or pooping as the sensation of needing to eliminate waste. It becomes your job to develop this communication. Don't worry if you are unsure of how to do that—we will go over the steps

you need to take in the next
section.

Benefits of Establishing a Communication Connection during Toilet Training

- Your Toddler Can Tell You When They Need to Go- Even though the 2-day method requires you to spend every moment of the day with your child, you may miss a cue. They may sneak away to the corner to use the bathroom at first, or they simply might lack the mental connection that indicates the sensation they are feeling is needing to pee or poop. Once you teach them the words and connect them with the sensations they are experiencing by using elimination communication, however, most of the hard part of potty training is over.

- You Can Clearly Communicate Your Pride- Using the toilet is a huge deal for your toddler. When you toilet train earlier, you have the advantage of still working with a toddler who is receptive to making you happy. Rather than being defiant and resistant, the communication you develop will encourage them to share in the happiness with you and do what you want them to.

- You Can Encourage Your Child to Share and Ask Questions- While going to the bathroom is simple for adults, it can seem intimidating to a toddler. When you have open communication, your toddler feels comfortable asking questions and sharing the way that their body is feeling. This increases the chance of success.

- You Build Your Relationship with Your Toddler- Your child is going to look to you for guidance during this major milestone in their life. This is especially true for older children, who have started to use the bathroom in their diapers and felt the sensations already. As you accomplish potty training together, the connection and communication between you and your toddler will strengthen your relationship.

How to Connect with Your Child for Potty Training

Elimination communication is critical to potty training success, especially for younger children who are still identifying their bodily sensations and how they relate to eliminating waste. To form a solid communication connection that will form the foundation for toilet training, use the following steps.

1. Educate Your Child through Observation- One of the easiest ways to start teaching your child about the potty is to take them along with you when you use the toilet. Make grunting noises while you are pooping and after you finish, let them see it in the bowl. Toddlers tend to follow their parents to the bathroom anyway, so don't resist next time. Be sure to communicate what you are doing, using phrases like pee, poop, and 'going potty.' Also,

don't forget to wash your hands afterward!

2. Rely on the Power of Media-Toddlers are very visual learners, because one of the things that they can easily relate to their senses is what they are seeing. For this reason, movies, books and television shows are all useful tools when it comes to toilet training your little one. They can often explain areas where parents are unclear or confusing to their little one. If your child doesn't seem to be as interested in the basic potty training media, consider finding shows with their favorite characters to teach them how to go. Some well-known books and movies are by Sesame

Street, Dora, Daniel Tiger and Caillou. Others involve princesses, superheroes, or just the average girl or boy. If you fancy a project, work together with your child to describe the process and create your own potty training book. Another great choice are baby dolls that 'pee' or 'poop' in their pants. Use them to teach your child about where pee and poop comes out and where they need to go when they eliminate waste.

3. Watch for Specific Indicators- For each child, there is usually a telltale sign that indicates they need to use the bathroom. This could include moving around, holding their private areas,

hiding in a corner or making a specific sound. By paying attention to these indicators, you can help your toddler understand the relationship between the way they are feeling and needing to go on the toilet for elimination.

4. Encourage Your Child to Communicate Their Ideas and Experience- About a year after our oldest was potty trained, he became obsessed with tacking the word 'poop' onto everything. He could be saying worse things, but it bothered me that he had developed such a 'potty' mouth. While your child is learning to use the toilet, however, there is nothing wrong with this type of talk. Encourage your child to talk

about their experience and share thoughts about the way they are feeling when they need to use the bathroom. Being encouraging and receptive to whatever they say about the toilet training process will open the channels of communication and encourage them to share more. This is critical for potty training success.

5. Keep Potty Training Talk Positive- One of the biggest mistakes that parents make when potty training is making it seem as if having an accident is a big deal. The 2-day method can become frustrating, especially if you choose to go with the generally more effective 'no underwear' route. Do not make a

big deal about messes—just clean them up. Then, when you can, put the mess into the toilet and explain to your child that he or she should make those types of messes in the potty from now on. Making your toddler feel ashamed about accidents is not just discouraging—it can create negative associations with the toilet training process and cause them to take longer to potty train.

6. Make Sure They Know You Are Proud- As you are minimizing accidents, you should also be praising your toddler each time that they are successful on the potty. Offer plenty of praise and affection and make sure they know that you are proud of their

accomplishments on the toilet. This positive reinforcement will make your toddler feel good about what they are doing on the potty and you will feel good about it, too.

CHAPTER SUMMARY:

1.   Successful elimination communication means simply that there is an open channel of communication between yourself and your toddler. He or she should become more comfortable communicating their emotions about potty training, as well as when they need to go. You also must communicate your expectations with your toddler in

a positive way, both as you are preparing and during the potty training process. Another part of good communication is being receptive, by responding to your toddler's questions and ensuring they are responsive to the positive feedback you are giving them when they go on the toilet.

2. There are many benefits of establishing open channels of communication between yourself and your child in all areas of parenting. When used for potty training, elimination communication helps clarify times when your child needs to pee or poop, makes your child feel your confidence and pride, encourages your toddler to share

and ask questions, and improves your relationship overall.

3. There are several steps that go into developing positive potty training communication between yourself and your child. These include providing the right tools and materials for observation and helping your child learn what to do, watching for indicators that your toddler needs to use the toilet, providing plenty of positive communication and downplaying accidents. By doing these things, you will foster good communication and make the potty training process significantly easier on both of you.

YOUR QUICK START ACTION STEP: START COMMUNICATING ABOUT POTTY TRAINING

It is never too early to start familiarizing your toddler with what happens on the potty. Encourage them to share bathroom time with you and learn about peeing and pooping, through observation and the many media options available. It is also a good time to introduce materials like potty training books and movies. These things and plenty of talking about the weekend that is coming up are essential to getting your communication channels open and preparing for the upcoming lessons.

Chapter 4: Toilet Introduction

Chapter 4: Toilet Introduction

This chapter is going to be the first action step in introducing your child to the toilet. While some ideas were provided in the previous chapter, this will go more into depth about how you should introduce your toddler to the toilet.

Understanding the Toilet: What Your Toddler Needs to Know

How you introduce the toilet to your child is critical to potty training failure or success. There are several areas that you should address, including:

- Where Waste Goes- The major goal of potty training is teaching your toddler where pee and poop are supposed to go. Some parents have fun teaching their child that the toilet is 'eating' their waste, but this can be scary to some. Use your best judgment to decide what will work best with your toddler.
- Who Goes on the Potty- When you are amping up your child for going to the restroom, it may be a good idea to show them

television shows or books where their favorite characters eliminate waste in the toilet. You could also praise older children (like an older sibling or cousin) who uses the big potty and how proud their parents must be. By giving your child role models that they want to be like and relating this to going to the toilet, your child will want to eliminate waste on the toilet as well.

- Wiping- While getting your toddler to go in the toilet is the major milestone that you are trying to meet, familiarizing them with wiping at this stage can be very helpful later, once they have mastered using the potty.

- Bathroom Hygiene- In addition to the basics of using the toilet, you should teach your child bathroom hygiene. Be sure to emphasize washing hands each time that your toddler uses the potty, especially if he or she enjoys washing their hands.

Benefits of the Pre-Game Warm up

One of the reasons that we were skeptical about the 2-day method with our daughter was because it did not seem possible that she could learn in such a short time. It is more practical, however, to think of the two days that you are heavily focusing on toilet training as a sort of boot camp and remember that the pre-game warm up is important as the actual game. It helps prep your toddler, so when the big weekend does come, they are more than ready to show you what they can do. Here are some of the benefits of preparing your child well before the weekend:

- It Starts Shaping Your Child's Expectations- When you are collaborating with someone else, one of the most common reasons for disappointment is unclear expectation. When you consistently relate peeing and pooping to the bathroom and provide positive feedback when he or she shows an interest, they become familiar with the potty training process and what is expected of them.

- You Have Time to Promote the Idea- The 2-day method is incredibly effective for children who are ready—but you must ensure your toddler is ready before the weekend happens for it to be a success. By introducing the idea before your toddler is put to the test, you give them time to get familiar with the idea.

- You Can Let Your Child Pick Their Tools- Letting your child choose their potty chair or picking out underwear with their favorite character on them can be incredibly beneficial as an incentive to get the job done. It may provide just the motivation that they need to propel them toward success. Additionally, by letting your child pick out new undies and a potty chair to use, it helps build the excitement for the weekend to come.

- It Lets You Determine if Your Child is Really Ready- There are some people who will tell you that regardless of what you do, you cannot force a child who is not ready. However, the people who say that are often working with older children who have started to show their individuality and defiance. They may fight against each of their parents' attempts at training them because they have already become accustomed to doing whatever they want and just using their diaper when they have to go. When you are dealing with a younger child, as you often are when using this earlier method of potty training, it is more likely that it will be effective. Additionally, by pre-gaming and exploring the idea of potty training before the big weekend, you can use your own judgment as to if your little one is ready to start using the toilet.

Steps for Effective Toilet Introduction

As you get started, be sure to keep the following steps in mind:

1. Let Them Accompany You to the Bathroom- If you listen to any parent, they may tell you that trying to go to the bathroom alone is a nightmare. When you are considering potty training, however, use this to your advantage. Show your little one how to go on the potty by making encouraging noises and explaining what you are doing. You can also let them observe older siblings, when appropriate.

2. Decide on a Method of Education- As mentioned earlier, there are several ways to educate your child about toilet training. You can find books or movies dedicated to potty training or use a 'potty' baby doll. By education

your little one, you will answer questions that they may not know how to ask yet. Remember that curiosity is a good thing. It shows that using the bathroom has piqued your child's interest.

3. Buying Their Own Potty- As you choose a toilet, you have the option of picking one that sits on the ground or one that sits on top of the toilet seat in your bathroom, along with a stool so your toddler can get up to the toilet. The one that sits on top of the toilet can be a good option if it seems he or she is interested in using the toilet where you go. The ones that sit on the floor, however, have the advantage of being portable so you can set

them in whatever room your child is in and quickly get them to the potty. You can also choose to invest in both.

4. Choosing Underwear- 'Big girl' or 'big boy' underwear are a great incentive for children learning to potty train. If you do decide that you do not want to use the 'no underpants' method, then you should have your child choose two types of underwear—some plain undies with a little extra padding for the weekend of training and some character underwear to use as a reward once your toddler has been successful at potty training.

CHAPTER SUMMARY:

1. There are several things that you should familiarize your little one with before beginning their potty training journey. This includes demonstrating how to use the potty, educating them with media and other materials, introducing wiping, and encouraging good bathroom hygiene.

2. When you take the time to warm-up your toddler to the idea of toilet training before their big weekend, you make it more likely that they will have success. The benefits of doing this include establishing expectations, giving your child time to think about the idea and ask questions, allowing

them to pick their underwear and toilet, and helping you decide if you and your toddler are ready for potty training boot camp.

3. The steps provided in this chapter will help make introducing the toilet easier. This is a critical step before moving onto potty training boot camp. The best way to do this is through demonstration, sharing of the ideas of potty training, and choosing a toilet and 'big' kid underwear.

YOUR QUICK START ACTION STEP: SCHEDULE POTTY TRAINING LEARNING TIMES

Get out your calendar now and write down the date that you should have your child familiarized with the toilet. Ideally, you should finish doing this the week prior to potty training boot camp. This is far enough from the date to get them excited, but close enough that they will stay excited as they anticipate the important weekend to come.

Chapter 5: How to Apply the Two-Day Method

Chapter 5: How to Apply the Two-Day Method

After reading the previous chapters, you should be almost ready to get started on the 2-day method of toilet training. This will go over the plan in depth, so you know exactly what to expect over the weekend.

Why the 2-Day Method Works

The basic principles behind the 2-day method are similar to the more popular 3-day method. However, for parents that work during the week, it is a lot more convenient and easier to apply than a method that takes three days.

The 2-day method works because you spend plenty of time getting your child familiar with the toilet and what is expected of him or her. Once you have done this, your toddler is mentally prepared to take the next step.

One of the key components of a successful 2-day boot camp for potty training is having a child who is willing to please their parents. This is the reason that it is typically recommended that younger children (between 1 and 2) are trained using this method. You may have success for other ages, but it may be more difficult because the child has already developed their own attitude. They also have learned to ignore their bodily urges or go in their diaper because it is convenient.

Finally, you will notice that the 2-day method emphasizes letting your little one run around without underpants on. This is the best technique because it teaches them the sensations associated with peeing and pooping. The speed that it works at makes it convenient since you can do it over the weekend or on a short family vacation.

Benefits of the 2-Day Method

As mentioned before, following the steps provided are essential to potty training success. There are numerous benefits that come along with this method. Here is a brief reminder:

- It is a no-hassle way to potty train since toddlers quickly learn what is expected of them.
- You can move straight from diapers to underwear, eliminating the need for expensive pull-ups.
- By training at a younger age, you lessen your impact on the

environment because of disposable diapers, without having to scrub cloth diapers for the next couple years of your child's life.

- Children are generally less defiant and more eager to please, so they will be easier to communicate with about the potty.

- The 2-day method also quickly boosts your child's self-esteem, confidence, and independence, because it sets them up for success (and plenty of praise from you).

- It is a quick method of training that can be done

in a single weekend, which is great for busy families.

How to Potty Train in 2 Days

Now that you have all the background knowledge needed, here is the most effective way to train your toddler to use the potty in just two days:

Step 1: Say Bye to the Diaper

Day One of potty training boot camp starts off as your child gets out of bed. Hand him or her a drink to start the day and walk them to the garbage can. Have them remove their diaper, put it in the can, and say goodbye. Do not give them the option of wearing a diaper for the rest of the weekend.

Step 2: Give an Explanation

Shortly after, explain to your toddler why you are not putting a diaper on them. You can let them run around naked or put them in a long nighty or t-shirt. Just be sure to keep their bottom exposed. Then, lead them over to the toilet and encourage them to try it out. Explain that they will not have a diaper to catch their mess for the day, so the potty is where it needs to go.

Step 3: Have Breakfast

Next, sit down for breakfast. Let your child have another drink. Shortly after you have finished eating (or sooner if they indicate they need to go), take your toddler to the potty. This is likely to be a successful trip since it has followed two drinks and a meal.

Step 4: Stop at Regular Intervals for Reminders

The next two days, you will stay in the house and follow this routine. The best thing to do is take your child every 15 minutes, especially if you are trying to avoid an accident. Each time that he or she is successful do not forget to give plenty of praise and affection, along with the reward that you have chosen for your child.

Step 5: Slow Down on Drinks about an Hour before Sleep

As it approaches your toddler's naptime, cut off the drinks. Make sure to put him or her to bed after a successful toilet attempt. Some will recommend training for the day and night at different times, but it is least confusing if you do not put a diaper back on your child for the entire potty training boot camp. You will want to repeat this ceasing of liquids and foods about an hour before bed at night. Make sure your little one uses the bathroom before going to bed and put down a plastic mattress cover if you are overly concerned about accidents.

Step 6: Wake Your Little One at Night

About half way through the night, you will want to set the alarm to wake your toddler up to go potty. This is a trip that you and he/she will not enjoy, but it is necessary to help train their body to wake up and potty, rather than just going in a diaper and staying in the wetness all night.

Step 7: Do it Again the Next Day

Follow the same ritual on the second day, encouraging your little one to go often and pushing the drinks. You will be surprised how quickly they catch on. Once Monday rolls around, they will be more than ready to don their 'big' kid underwear and handle the day.

Bonus Step: Remember to Stay Positive

Expect your child to have accidents, even if you walk him or her to the toilet every 15 minutes. When it happens, calmly clean the mess and explain where he/she should be eliminating waste. Keep your attitude calm and positive. When they do pee or poop, remember what a big deal it is to them (and you). Celebrate each of their successes and in no time, you will have a positively potty trained toddler.

CHAPTER SUMMARY:

1. The 2-day method is most effective on toddlers who are eager to please their parents and who have not yet developed the habit of sitting in a soiled diaper. By preparing your child and introducing them to the toilet before the actual boot camp, you set them up for success.

2. Remember that your child's success will come with many benefits. It can be tough to fit a whole weekend in where you just stay at home with your toddler, but it is well worth it as you boost your child's independence and lower your cost of diapers and impact on the environment.

3. By following the steps provided in this chapter, you ultimately set your toddler up for potty training success. Offer plenty of drinks and make your little one say goodbye to their diaper—even for nap time and bedtime. Take them to the bathroom regularly, even in the middle of the night, and don't forget to react positively each time that they go to the bathroom where they are supposed to.

YOUR QUICK START ACTION STEP: SCHEDULE A WEEKEND TO GET IT DONE

Now that you have all the information you need for success, it is time to get the job done. Schedule a weekend you can stay home with your toddler and follow the steps outlined in this chapter. If you want a little extra help, read the next couple chapters for extra advice before you get started.

Chapter 6:
How to Apply
a
Diaper-Free
Solution

Chapter 6: How to Apply a Diaper-Free Solution

In this chapter, we will go over how to get your potty trained toddler out of a diaper for good. You will also learn what this means and the major benefits that your toddler gets when switching from diapers or pull-ups to underwear.

What Does Diaper-Free Mean?

Diaper-free means that you will never have to spend money on a pack of diapers or pull-ups again.

You should feel confident enough in your toddler's abilities (and they should feel confident in their own abilities) that they can wear underwear all the time.

The expectation of being diaper-free is that your child will go to the bathroom in the toilet regularly. Note that this does not mean he or she will not have any accidents. Even toddlers who have been potty trained for a year or more can have the occasional mess in their pants. Here are some examples of diaper-free kids.

Katelyn is starting her first day of preschool and she must be potty trained. After a crash course over the weekend about 2 weeks before school, she started to use the toilet regularly. Even though she has been doing well, Katelyn has two accidents on the first day of school. This is a big transition for her, however, so the teacher is understanding. By the end of the first week of school, Katelyn is making it through the day without messing in her pants. She is considered diaper-free.

Jonathan is two-years old and has impressed his parents with his potty training efforts. Though he does not wear diapers during the day, he is still frequently wetting the bed at night. His mother decides to use thickly padded underwear at night to try and contain the mess. Even though needs the extra protection at night, Jonathan is still considered diaper-free.

Benefits of Being Diaper-Free

When you start toilet training your toddler, the major goal is getting them to regularly eliminate waste in the toilet. Being diaper-free means consistently avoiding diapers. This is important because it prevents regression, or, going back to poor potty training habits. In addition to keeping your toddler on track for potty training, being diaper-free comes with several other benefits, including:

- Reassures Your Child of Your Trust and Pride- When you keep your toddler out of diapers, you are reinforcing the idea that you trust them to continue using the potty. They are also reassured of how proud you are of them, which reinforces the desire to continue using the toilet.

- Eliminates the Cost of Diapers Completely- Nighttime training pants and the occasional naptime diaper can be expensive, too. By being diaper-free, you eliminate the cost and the associated environmental impact completely.

- Prevents Regression- If you continue to put your child in diapers after the toilet training weekend, even for just naps or nighttime, it can send mixed signals. They may be less likely to learn to go while sleeping and will not pay attention to their body signals as much. In a worst-case scenario, they may also start to use the bathroom in their pants during the day, too. Staying away from diapers altogether helps prevent this.

Teaching Your Toddler to Be Diaper-Free

If potty training boot camp went well, then you already have a great start on getting your child to be diaper-free. Here is what you need to do.

Step 1: Teach Your Child to Pull Up and Down

Potty training boot camp involved keeping your little one out of underwear and diapers, so there is a chance they do not know how to pull their underwear up and down. Teach them this as part of the potty process and monitor them for the first couple days, ensuring they are moving fast enough to get the pee or poop in the toilet. You should also avoid anything with hard closures (like buttons, snaps, overalls, and onesies) once you have toilet trained your child.

Step 2: Commit to the Toilet Training Process

Once you have taught them to pull up and down, the only thing left to do is to commit to potty training fully. Do not put them in diapers or at night, or when you leave the house. Try to plan outings around being somewhere near a potty for the first week or two, or plan to make frequent stops to let your little one use the bathroom.

Step 3: Clean Messes—Don't Contain Them

If you are striving to be completely diaper-free, then you should expect messes. Try not to get upset—otherwise, your child can quickly become discouraged and give up altogether. You also should not use diapers at all. Trying to contain the mess will just teach your toddler that it is okay to eliminate in their pants sometimes.

https://www.verywellfamily.com/potty-training-problems-not-pooping-on-the-potty-2634549

https://www.thebump.com/a/potty-training-how-to-get-started-and-making-it-work

CHAPTER SUMMARY:

1. Diaper-free training involves having a child that is diaper-free, day and night. This can take some time after potty training boot camp, but you must stay committed to it. Otherwise, your toddler may start to have accidents.

2. When you choose not to use a diaper on your child, you reassure them of your trust and confidence in them. Additionally, you eliminate the environmental impact and the cost of diapers. Finally, going diaper-free

completely helps prevent regression.

3. There are a few steps you will need to take after the 2-day toilet training session to ensure your little one remains diaper-free. You should teach him or her to pull their underwear up and down, stay consistent with toilet training, and avoid using diapers altogether.

YOUR QUICK START ACTION STEP: BRUSH UP ON TIPS FOR BEING DIAPER-FREE

Now that you have an idea of how to create a completely diaper-free life for your child visit at least one website to find tips that may help you achieve this goal.

Chapter 7: Potty Training: Mistakes to Avoid

Chapter 7: Potty Training: Mistakes to Avoid

If you are a first time parent or just one who didn't quite nail potty training the first time around, you should know that mistakes happen. It is not a judgment of your parenting skill, nor does it mean you are destined for toilet training failure. The best way to avoid these mistakes is to get educated on what they are, so you can work at avoiding them.

What Are Toilet Training Mistakes?

Potty training mistakes are usually small things that you might not think of as being a problem. However, even things that seem insignificant can set your child back.

For example, Jeff's mom decided to potty train him before starting a new school. They moved to a new house the following weekend and Jeff started to have frequent accidents. Jeff's mom wonders if her methods were ineffective. The problem with this scenario is not Jeff or his mother—it is the move. Moving to a new home is a stressful life event and Jeff may have been set back by the experience.

Another example is Kristy. Kristy did amazing at boot camp, but when her family returned to their schedule the next week, she started having accidents. This likely happened because Kristy just was not ready to pay attention to her bowel movements on her own yet. She is not receiving the same attention following the weekend, so the ideas they spent creating are not being reinforced.

Why You Need to Know These Mistakes

As with many things in life, the best offense is a good defense. By knowing what the most common mistakes are and how to look for them, you can easily set you and your child up for toilet training success.

Know that these are not the only mistakes you can make, but they are the most common. Also, feel assured that these mistakes can happen to anyone—what really matters is having the strength to overcome them. Here are some of the benefits of being familiar with potty training mistakes:

- You can quickly respond to mistakes, once you identify what is causing them.
- You can prevent setbacks by quickly responding to mistakes.
- You know what to look for, should an unexpected problem arise.
- You can troubleshoot the toilet training process, especially if you are not sure the reason your toddler is struggling.

How to Avoid Potty Training Mistakes

1. Keep Your Child Hydrated

One of the biggest reasons potty training fails is because the peeing or pooping sensation is not distinct enough for children to notice it. To ensure their signals are strong enough, make sure they drink plenty of drinks throughout the weekend. Use reduced sugar (or watered down) juice to keep them hydrated.

2. Do Not Train During Times of Stress

Things like moving, getting a new pet, or starting school can be excited and fun. However, they also are not the best time to toilet train. When a child is focusing on outside factors that cause stress, whether positive or negative, it makes it hard to concentrate on their bodily sensations and if they need to use the restroom.

3. Do Not Freak Over Accidents

Once your child moves into the world of 'big boy' or 'big girl' underwear and bathroom habits, accidents are likely to happen. You may occasionally hear stories about a child who never wet his or her pants again after toilet training, but more than likely, there will be a few messes. Remember to handle these gracefully—they are natural and you do not want your child associating negative emotions with their body elimination.

4. Don't Go Back to Diapers

Following the 2-day toilet training boot camp, you should not encourage your child to use diapers any longer. Instead, make frequent stops on long car rides, plan your grocery store trips around which have potties inside, and actively work to keep your toddler dry and out of diapers. Parents who have toddlers that struggle with nighttime dryness may choose to use diapers at night. While this is not recommended, it may be a solution if your toddler is struggling with nighttime dryness.

CHAPTER SUMMARY:

1. Mistakes can happen to any parent who is training their toddler to use the toilet. Success comes from overcoming these struggles.

2. There are numerous benefits to recognizing the struggles that your child may face as they move from potty trained to completely diaper free. By expecting the occasional issue to arise, you can quickly respond to the mistakes and prevent regression and setbacks.

3. Identifying some of the mistakes that happen during the toilet training process can stop them from happening. Be sure to train at the right time, keep your child well-fed and hydrated,

avoid using diapers completely, and remain calm and supportive in the face of accidents.

YOUR QUICK START ACTION STEP:

While this information is sufficient for prevention of problems that commonly arise, you should still educate yourself on what else may go wrong. Do not scare yourself away from potty training, but do prepare yourself by looking up the do's and don'ts of toilet training.

Chapter 8:
Potty Training

—

Tips for Boys

Chapter 8: Potty Training – Tips for Boys

In this chapter, we will briefly focus on toilet training for boys. One of the major differences between toilet training boys and girls is that boys will need to be taught to stand and aim when they are ready. This chapter will go over what else you need to know.

Why You Need to Train Your Boy as a Boy

As you are training your child, you are teaching them a lot about their body. This makes it a good time to note that boys and girls are different. Developing 'boy' bathroom habits early will make it easier to teach him standing up later. This will be necessary to prevent 'missing' the toilet in the future. Some other benefits include:

- No Need to Re-Learn- Some boys feel more comfortable sitting on the potty to pee, especially when they are first learning. If they do learn to stand and pee first, however, they will not have to re-learn this new method of peeing later.

- Improved Aim- When your toddler has more practice, he will be able to aim better.

Toddler Potty Training Tips for Boys

- Give Him Something to Aim at- Small cheerios or other things that will float are a good choice for getting your son to pee inside the potty. Simply instruct him to hold his private area and aim at the designated item. Alternatively, place a sticker on the bottom of his toilet training chair.
- Teach Him to Feel Comfortable Holding His Penis- While we always

encourage children not to play with themselves in public, your son should feel comfortable holding himself and directing his stream where it needs to go. This is a great job for an older brother, dad, or an uncle to teach.

- Choose a Sitting Potty with a 'Lip'- Some children's toilets have a small hump or cup in the front, which is designed to catch your little one's flow if it shoots over the edge of the seat while he is toilet training.

CHAPTER SUMMARY:

1. Boys and girls are different, especially because boys will eventually need to learn to stand and pee.

2. Allowing your boy to learn in a 'boy-specific' toilet training manner will help prevent future struggles.

3. Some of the tips that you should employ while teaching your little boy to use the bathroom include giving him something to aim at, teaching him to hold his private parts, and using a potty that has a cup or lip, to catch stray urine while he is sitting to poop.

YOUR QUICK START ACTION STEP: PLAN A 'BOY' TRAINING CAMP

Use the tips provided here to help make potty training more effective for your little boy, if you are trying to train your son. These tips are something not all parents think about and will make toilet training much simpler.

Chapter 9:
Potty Training
– Tips for
Girls

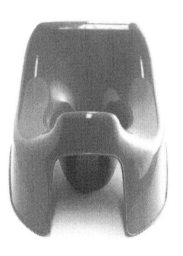

Chapter 9: Potty Training – Tips for Girls

In this chapter, we will discuss a few girl-specific tips. The major difference between girls and boys is that girls must learn how to wipe appropriately. This chapter will teach you more about this, as well as some bonus tips for training your little girl.

Why You Need to Potty Train Your Girl as a Girl

There are two major distinctions between boys and girls. The first is whether they sit or stand to pee and the second is wiping. Wiping can become a hygiene issue if it is not done properly. You must train your little girl to wipe from front to back and to clean every time that she pees. The benefits include:

- Less Chance of Infection- If your toddler is not wiping the right way, it can lead to irritation and infection in her private area. Proper wiping can prevent this.
- Better Cleanliness- Girls require more tact when it comes to cleaning after peeing than boys do. Getting them on the right

track earlier means more
cleanliness sooner.

Toddler Potty Training Tips for Girls

- Control Her Spray- Little
  girls can also have a
  problem with spraying
  over the front of the toilet.
  To prevent this, have your
  toddler sit with her knees
  slightly apart and back far
  enough that both her
  bottom and her private
  parts are over the toilet.

- Use a Potty Chair- For girls
  to pee, their pelvic muscles
  will need to relax and let
  the urine flow. It is easier
  to do this on a potty chair,

where your daughter's feet can touch the floor.

- Encourage Proper Wiping from the Beginning- Teach your daughter to wipe until she feels dry. You should also teach her to wipe from front to back, which will prevent infection and irritation.

CHAPTER SUMMARY:

1. The major difference between toilet training girls vs. boys is how they sit/stand and the aftercare.

2. Recognizing this difference is critical to proper hygiene and toilet training success. It will also

prevent infection caused by improper wiping.

3. By following tips like ensuring your toddler is positioned properly, teaching her to wipe properly, and using a toilet that sits close to the ground, you can improve your toddler's chance of toilet training success.

YOUR QUICK START ACTION STEP: PLAN FOR TRAINING YOUR LITTLE GIRL

If you have a little girl, implement the tips provided in this chapter into your toilet training plan. This will increase the chance of success.

BONUS Chapter: Helpful Tips for Dads

BONUS Chapter: Helpful Tips for Dads

The dads who potty train usually get less recognition than moms, because most people associate it with being a 'mom's' job. The ones that do, however, are real champs. Dads are typically portrayed as wanting to avoid messes. However, many take the mess that comes along with toilet training in stride and can have a sense of humor that mom might not. Here are some tips for dads who are taking on the responsibility of toddler potty training.

Why Dads Deserve (and Need) Potty Training Tips

Much of the material designed for potty training is geared toward moms, who are often credited for handling the messes that come along with raising a child, toilet training included. Even so, dads who take advantage of toilet training tips get the following benefits:

- A Better Idea of What to Expect- When you learn what tips can help you as a father trying to toilet train, you are giving yourself the advantage of knowing what is to come so you can prepare better.

- Unique Approach- Moms and dads are known for their different approaches to discipline, play time, snacking—really everything. Potty training should not be excluded from this, especially if your toddler responds better to a dad's approach.

Toilet Training Tips for Dad

- Develop a Sense of Humor- Things are going to get 'messy' over your potty training weekend. It can be easy to freak out, especially if you are usually the one handling your toddler's messes.

Even so, it is important to remain calm and collected in the face of messes and learn to laugh off what your child does. Potty training becomes a lot easier and more fun if you have a sense of humor to tackle it with.

- Come Up with a Code- Is there a particular animal you can get your child interested in? Snakes work well because they look like the shape that is often left in the toilet after a poop. Even if your toddler isn't into snakes, though, come up with a cool 'victory' call that you can use each time that they poop in the potty.

This is a fun dad-worthy technique.

- Stock Up on Area Rugs- If you really want to avoid cleaning up messes, buy some extra area rugs. You won't have to scrub too hard and you will not have to worry about losing your security deposit. Get the ones with rubber backing for extra security— especially if you want to let him or her sit on the furniture.

CHAPTER SUMMARY:

1. Even though people usually associate childcare, diaper changing, and potty training with

moms, dads often have a unique approach that can be beneficial to their toddler.

2. When you check out potty training tips especially for dads, you find tips that match up with your personality. This can help you learn what to expect and help develop a potty training technique that fits perfectly with your toddler's learning abilities.

3. Having dad-friendly tips can make the toilet training process significantly easier. This includes using rubber-backed area rugs to prevent messes or staining, creating a victory cry, and having a sense of humor about toddler toilet training.

YOUR QUICK START ACTION STEP: COME UP WITH A PLAN

If you are a dad reading this chapter, then good luck as you tackle potty training with your toddler. Be sure to implement these tips as part of your plan if you believe they may make the process easier.

Conclusion

Thank you again for owning this book!

I hope this book was able to help you learn the best methods for potty training your toddler. Whether your toddler is a girl or boy, you should now be armed with the knowledge to make toilet training happen in just two days. From there, you will be able to encourage your child to go completely diaper-free and avoid potty training mistakes.
The next step is to come up with a plan and put it into action. With the knowledge you now have, the only thing left is to get the potty training weekend done.

Finally, if this book has given you value and helped you in any way, then I'd like to ask you for a favor. If you would be kind enough to leave a review for this book on Amazon, it'd be greatly appreciated!

Thank you and good luck!

.

80361044R00091

Made in the USA
San Bernardino, CA
26 June 2018